CW00386401

Let God be God

Let God be God

SONGS OF HOPE AND CONSOLATION

Faith Cook

PUBLISHING WITH A MISSION

EP BOOKS
Faverdale North
Darlington
DL3 0PH, England

web: http://www.epbooks.org

e-mail: sales@epbooks.org

First published 2012

British Library Cataloguing in Publication Data available

ISBN: 978-0-85234-850-5

Printed and bound in Great Britain by the MPG Books Group, Bodmin and King's Lynn.

*C*ontents

An explanation

Most of the verses contained in this book were composed during a twenty-year period between 1980–2000. Some arose out of material I was reading in connection with the biographical accounts I was working on at the time. The majority, however, were written as a direct result either of sermons that had influenced me, books that I was reading or as an expression of God's personal dealings with me in correction, encouragement and comfort. The quotations accompanying the lines are also largely drawn from books I have read that have stimulated and shaped my thinking.

From time to time a number of friends have asked me if I would be willing to allow these verses, some of a quite personal nature, to be published. It is only the desire that others may find hope and consolation through these lines that has eventually persuaded me to do so.

I owe my warm thanks to Dr Jack Milner for many of the evocative photographs included in this book.

Let God be God

Amid the broken hopes of earth,
assailed by doubt, bowed low by care,
I battled long, nor found relief
till faith could triumph and declare:
'My God is good, I surely know,
come pain, come loss, come shock or woe.'

Should sorrow blight my fairest flower,
should anguish pierce with keenest thrust,
should sword or tribulation strike
to cast life's treasures to the dust,
not all can sever me from Christ,
and Christ for me shall all-suffice.

Upon the ashes of my hope
this monument my faith shall raise,
LET GOD BE GOD — it is enough —
and God is right in all his ways.
Then let me trust although he slay,
till flees my night, till dawns THE DAY.

The
God of grace

Surprising grace

There must be few believers who have not at some time felt a degree of total astonishment that the grace of God was ever shown to them, and particularly so in a generation such as our own. I wrote these lines late one night following a Bible exposition on the words of Philippians 3:12: 'That I may lay hold of that for which Christ Jesus has also laid hold of me.' They express the strong desire to return some token of thanks to the Saviour for the undeserved love and mercy shown so freely to a sinner.

*M*y God, how shall I tell the grace,
or how the tender mercy trace
that looked upon a fallen race
and then laid hold on me?

The mighty angels stood amazed;
the seraphim in wonder gazed,
then loud their gladdest anthems raised
when Christ laid hold on me!

Who, who can plumb the mystery?
No tongue can tell: then let me be
surprised to all eternity
that Christ laid hold on me!

And how may I such love return?
O let my soul with passion burn
while prostrate at his feet I learn
why Christ laid hold on me.

To know him more would I aspire,
to love him with a heart of fire,
wrapped up in him, my one desire,
who first laid hold on me.

Then onward to that mark I press
till I the heavenly prize possess,
and with the ransomed throng confess,
'My Christ laid hold on me!'

How great are the privileges which result from an ability to say, 'Christ is mine'. If Christ is yours, then all that he possesses is yours. His power is yours to defend you; his wisdom and knowledge are yours to guide you; his righteousness is yours to justify you; his Spirit and grace are yours to sanctify you; his heaven is yours to receive you. He is as much yours as you are his, and as he requires all that you have to be given to him, so he gives all that he has to you. Come to him then with holy boldness and take what is your own!

Edward Payson's *Remains*, Religious Tract Society, 1828, p. 91

Unseen yet loved

William Williams (1717–1791), called the Sweet Singer of Wales, wrote at least 850 hymns during the eighteenth-century evangelical revival. Most were in Welsh, a few in English and others translated into English. The following lines, transliterated from the Welsh, read:

*I*nvisible One, I love you,
wonderful is the power of your grace
pulling my soul so sweetly
away from its choicest pleasures.
You did more in one brief minute
than the whole world ever did,
winning for yourself a quiet seat
in this heart of stone.

Rendering these lines fairly freely, I wrote the following, expressing the astonishing grace of God to an undeserving sinner.

*U*nseen yet loved, my God, my friend,
I sing the wonders of your grace,
who in this stubborn heart of stone
has won a quiet resting place.

Sweetly from earth's beguiling charms
you drew my restless soul away;
in one bright moment heaped on me
ten thousand blessings more than they.

I cannot love you, Lord, enough;
then may a sinner, dearly bought,
here gaze and weep before your throne
at grace beyond the scope of thought.

I would sum up my present desires in two words: Love Christ! Love Christ!
Love Christ! He that does so will please God in the loveliest way and reach
heaven by the sweetest road.

From the writings of John Macdonald (1807–47)

Loved beyond measure

Why should anything have my heart but God, but Christ? He loves me, he loves me with love that passes knowledge. He loves me and he shall have me: he loves me and I will love him: his love stripped him of all for my sake; Lord, let my love strip me of all for your sake. I am a son of love, an object of love, a monument of love, of distinguishing love, of peculiar love, and of love that passes knowledge: and why should I not walk in love?

John Bunyan
The Saints Knowledge of Christ's love, Works, vol.2, p. 39

*H*ow often have they told me,
  this earth is passing fair;
  the hand of the Creator
  is printed everywhere.

But now in vision brighter
of realms before unknown,
  I see the Christ of glory
the Man upon the throne.

Tell me of earth no longer,
tell me of earth no more —
  his loveliness surpasses
creation's choicest store.

And yet he left the brightness
of his pure home on high,
and here alone in darkness,
  for me, yes me, to die.

Such love I cannot measure,
nor mind can comprehend;
the best of earth can never,
such matchless love transcend.

Surpassing love of Jesus,
my life-long song shall be;
and it shall be my anthem
to all eternity.

Unbounded, uncreated,
Unmeasured, full and free,
the mighty love of Jesus,
it could no greater be!

The above lines, based on thoughts in a long poem by a John Macdonald (1926) who cannot now be traced, tell of the measureless love of the Saviour — love beyond anything that this created world can offer or holds dear.

A welcome guest

How often believers find the Lord's Supper to be an occasion when they feel most cast down over their sins and sometimes assailed by Satan's vicious temptations. Only the remembrance of the grace of the suffering Saviour and his mercy to his people can silence the accusations of Satan.

*T*o his table richly spread
Christ invites his people near:
but I see his hands, his side
scarred by nail wounds and the spear.

Shamed with conscious guilt I come,
grieving as I learn to trace
all that my redemption cost
written on his patient face.

How may I partake the feast,
I, who daily still offend?
How may I who caused his pain
call the Son of God my friend?

Mercy shines within his eyes,
mercy rests upon his face,
mercy cancels all my debt,
by the merits of his grace.

Penitent I gladly come
to his feast — a welcome guest —
drink of Christ and share his life,
leaning on his kindly breast.

till at last I heav'nward rise,
all the work of grace complete,
taste of glory's undimmed wine,
love and worship at his feet.

The Lord Jesus is present at his own table... Look towards him with the assurance that he is just as tender and compassionate and forgiving as when he was on earth; and that he is the most accessible being in the universe... Rejoice that he knows all things and looks to the very bottom of your heart. Confide to him your deepest sense of unworthiness and of your unfitness for this privilege and flee to his righteousness in this solemn moment as fully covering all your sins. Guard against the supposition that your acceptance is dependent on feelings of joy or even comfort at his table... Go out of yourself and place your whole heart in his hands. If your thoughts wander or become confused, if you find yourself suddenly cold or hard or even bereft of all right feelings, avoid struggles of mind to repair the damage, but gently bring your thoughts to the all-gracious present Jesus who sees and pities your infirmities.

J. W. Alexander, *Remember Him*
Banner of Truth Trust, 2000, p. 21

Hope for
the penitent
and broken

Remember me

Adolph Saphir, a preacher in Notting Hill, London, and a close friend of C. H. Spurgeon, was from a Jewish family in Budapest. He was converted as a child under 'Rabbi' John Duncan whose short ministry there between 1841–43 was remarkably blessed. In Saphir's first book, *Conversion*, he describes the faith of the thief, crucified with Christ, who cried out in dying, 'Lord, remember me when you come into your kingdom.'

Wonderful was the prayer of the dying thief, but still more wonderful is the reply of Christ. He had remained silent when false witnesses rose up against him. When Herod wished to see some miracle done by him and questioned him with many words, he answered him nothing. When Pilate asked, 'What is truth?' Christ did not speak ... But scarcely had this poor sinner asked his favour and intercession when he delivered him from all uncertainty and fear by his word of power and love. Jesus was suffering unspeakable agony, yet even then his heart was full of sympathy, compassion and tenderness. Not for a moment can he forget the great work of salvation which his Father has given him to do; that love which glows in his heart for that Church which God had given him for his inheritance is so strong that even the floods of death cannot drown it — not even the agony of the cross can make him forget it.

Adolph Saphir, *Conversion*, 1870, p. 315

These words were written after hearing a message on this theme.

To Christ of Calvary I turn,
a sinner with no hope beside;
'Remember me,' my earnest cry,
O Son of God, the crucified.

Remember me in all life's stress
when numb with failure, pain and care,
or lured by Satan into wrong,
'Remember me,' is all my prayer.

Remember me when each day's tale
of weakness, stumbling, grieving, fear,
its wayward thoughts, its careless deeds,
before my troubled eyes appear.

When to the lonely bounds of life —
its dark, unknown extremity —
my faltering steps draw near at last,
then Saviour, Christ, 'Remember me'.

O stricken Lamb, before my eyes,
reveal your cross; my only plea,
that at my dying I may know
you always have remembered me.

When at your throne on that last day
this sin-sick world receives its due,
Say to my soul, O Judge of all,
'Fear not, I have remembered you.'

Repentance and hope

'There is hope in your future, says the LORD'

(Jeremiah 31:17).

Broken by my pain and sinning,
bowed beneath grief's crushing weight,
still I stumbled on in darkness:
solitary, desolate.
Nights of fierce regrets and weeping,
days of numb and bleak despair,
will the God of mercy listen,
heed my chastened, earnest prayer?

Will the God I long have trusted
speak forgiveness to my soul?
Can he lift the heavy burden,
make a wounded spirit whole?
Will the heart that bled to win me,
rescued me from Satan's power,
cast aside the one he's purchased,
leave me in an evil hour?

Steals upon my heart his answer,
'Child of mine, you shall not die;
hope lies hidden in your future,'
says the God who cannot lie:
hope beyond your expectations,
hope of joys as yet unborn,
hope when this sad night of weeping,
brightens to a better dawn.

Only trust him, child of glory,
trust his wise and perfect way,
bear with patience every sorrow,
through the dark and stormy day.
If the path prove yet more stony
firmer grasp his powerful hand,
hope in God, whose strength unfailing
will enable you to stand.

*B*lot out my transgressions

If you would hold Christ in your soul's embrace, keep grace in lovely exercise, keep the arm of faith continually about him; let the fire of divine love burn continually upon the altar of your heart; let the anchor of hope be fixed within the veil; let the fountain of evangelical repentance be continually running; and under your greatest attainments be humble, and take care to set the crown upon Christ's head, saying 'Not unto us, not unto us, but unto thy name be the glory.'

Ebenezer Erskine
Christ in the Believer's arms, Works, vol. 1, p. 176

*M*y God, and can you yet forgive
transgressors such as I?
Can mercy still avail for me
or pass my sinning by?
Each mild rebuke, each gentle word,
in folly I ignored,
nor dared esteem my ways and thoughts
displeasing to my Lord.

Yet still my path he hedged with love,
with grace on grace heaped high
(such understanding who can search,
such goodness magnify?)
until with kind severity
my God at length displayed
the sum of my iniquity,
in clarity arrayed.

I saw, I wept with stricken heart
before a chastening God,
then penitent I fled in haste
to Christ's effectual blood.
In streams of love from Jesu's heart
this fountain flows for me;
nor have I any hope beside
for my extremity.

Enough! my dying Friend, enough!
That blood has purged my stain
and to my pardoned spirit shown
a Father's smile again.
Here let me dwell and stray no more
beyond that cleansing flood;
Here only may I rest secure
close to the heart of God.

The Lord does not delight in his children's tears; he does not willingly afflict nor grieve the children of men; and yet he would rather have them cry than perish. Do not wonder, Christian, if your tender Lord allows you pain, and that your pains are so sharp and so many ... It is his mercy that he will chastise; you may put your corrections among his mercies. His breakings of you are his blessings, his woundings are your cures ... O my Lord, let me not lack your staff nor your rod.

Richard Alleine
Heaven Opened, Baker Book House, pp. 58-9

The true Christian is a penitent though a pardoned man. The length of his repentance is as long as his life. He daily repents because he daily offends. But his repentance is not so much out of fear as for unkindness... The wrong of his sins trouble him more than the danger.

William Grimshaw of Haworth

A Saviour's compassion

In Thomas Goodwin's treatise, *The Heart of Christ in Heaven towards Sinners on Earth,* he speaks of the unchangeable character of the Saviour who, though now exalted in heaven, is still as full of compassion for his people as he was during his earthly days.

> *Christ's heart in heaven, in respect of pity and compassion, remains the same as it was on earth; he intercedes there with the same heart as he did here below; and that he is as meek, as gentle, as easy to be entreated, as tender in his affections, so that they may deal with him as fairly about the great matter of their salvation and as hopefully and upon as easy terms to obtain it of him as they might if they might have been on earth with him, and be as familiar with him in all their needs.*

The Saviour's tears

Kind Son of God, did you on earth once weep
with your afflicted people here?
And flows there for your suff'ring children yet
a human tear?

Amid ten thousand shouts of holy joy
the ransomed shine in bliss unknown:
they weep no more — all tears are wiped away —
But yours alone.

Each sigh of mine, each stabbing shaft of pain
is borne upon the Saviour's heart;
though crowned with joy, the Man of Sorrows shares
the sufferer's part.

Then flow these eyes, then weep this bruisèd heart;
for Christ weeps too: the mourner's friend
still mingles tears of pity with my grief
till sorrows end.

Jesus, 'the Man of Sorrows, acquainted with grief' is the same divine person who has passed into the heavens, and there taken his place at the right hand of God, far above all principality and power. He once trod the same vale of tears which we now tread, and shared our feelings as well as our fortunes on earth; he stood by the bier of the widow's son; he groaned in spirit, and was troubled, wept at the grave of Lazarus and spoke soothingly to his weeping sisters. He it was who in his own person felt what it was to live a suffering life, and to die a painful death; and in the pangs of hunger and thirst, in the privations of poverty, in the perils of persecution, and in the deep agony of the garden and the cross, tasted every variety of human sorrow, and sounded the lowest depths of human nature.

The same divine person, who then suffered and wept, 'has passed into the heavens', but do not think that he has left his human sympathies behind him. There, as here, he is our High Priest … still: amidst the glories of the upper sanctuary, the same gracious work, and the same suffering people, engage his thoughts, as when he sojourned on earth.

Thomas Goodwin
The Heart of Christ in Heaven towards Sinners on earth
Works, 1862, vol. 2

Within the veil

The words of the following verses were written after hearing a sermon in which the preacher pointed out from the experience of Stephen, the first martyr of the Christian church, that the risen Saviour's compassion for his suffering people is so acute that when they are in desperate straits, and when they die, instead of remaining seated in his normal place at the Father's right hand, he rises from his throne and stands to encourage his people in their conflict, and to greet them when they come home to him.

'But he [Stephen], being full of the Holy Spirit, gazed into heaven and saw the glory of God, and Jesus standing at the right hand of God, and said, "Look! I see the heavens opened and the Son of Man standing at the right hand of God!"'

(Acts 7:55-56).

*S*eated at his Father's throne,
   interceding for his own,
Christ presents within the veil
prayers that ever must prevail.

Though I often heedless stray,
slight his laws, forsake his way,
   fear to share his lowly part,
love him with divided heart —
   still for me he lives and prays,
   still his tender grace displays;
      by his all-availing blood,
pleads a wanderer's cause with God.

But should sorrows press me sore,
Christ stays seated now no more;
   Jesus rises when he sees
   all my soul's extremities —
rises from his throne on high,
mindful of his children's cry;
   all his heart in pity moves,
   for the grief of those he loves.

Every pain, affliction, tear,
Jesus measures by his prayer,
bears my burden of distress
high upon his kindly breast.

When at death's appalling hour,
flesh must fail beneath its power,
Christ who broke that galling chain,
rises from his throne again;
stands to greet with smiling face
saints, long-loved, to his embrace;
calls the way-worn soul to come,
welcoming his pilgrim home.

John Bunyan, who had suffered much both at the hands of the tempter and through his long imprisonment, wrote these words in his moving work *The Doctrine of Law and Grace Unfolded*:

> *O had we not a Jesus at the right hand of God making intercession for us, and to convey fresh supplies of grace unto us through the virtue of his blood being pleaded at God's right hand, how soon would it be with us as it is with those for whom he prays not at all? But the reason why you stand while others fall, the reason why you go through the many temptations of the world, and shake them off from you while others are ensnared and entangled is because you have an interceding Jesus. 'I have prayed for you,' says he, 'that your faith fail not' (Luke 22:32).*

The
pilgrim way

All my days

The Lord has helped me all my days,
here will I stand.
Before time's dawn his tender love
my pathway planned;
Nor will he leave me till I reach
heaven's brighter land.

Though rough and long the pilgrim way
my steps have trod,
My guide still leads me safely on
by staff and rod,
all undismayed while still I cling
close to my God.

And should my path lead into night
or fears appall,
stayed on that mighty unseen arm
I need not fall;
while Christ is mine and I am his,
I still have all.

Should Jordan's flood before me spread
both deep and wide,
his power can cleave those gloomy depths
a path provide,
to bring my conqu'ring soul at last
to Jesu's side.

So shall I own my Father's care
with gladdest praise!
A monument of grateful love
I'll ever raise,
until I dwell at his right hand
through timeless days.

Faint not, the miles to heaven are but few and short ... therefore go on and let hope go before you. Sin not in your trials and victory is yours. Pray, wrestle and believe and you shall overcome as Jacob did. None can withstand you once you have prevailed with God.

Arise then, and set your foot up the mountain; go up out of the wilderness leaning on your Beloved. If you knew the welcome that awaits you when you reach home, you would hasten your pace; for you shall see your Lord put up his own holy hand to your face and wipe all tears from your eyes.

From the *Letters of Samuel Rutherford*

In spite of my murmurings, my faintings, my dullness, my deadness, my unbelief, God never left me but was ever with me. He supplied my wants, and many a time revived my fainting soul and did carry me as an eagle does her little ones ... Oh the care he had for me in the great wilderness [of this world], preserving me and carrying me through!

Mercies in the Wilderness
James Fraser of Brea

$\mathcal{N}ow$ ... and then

'For our light affliction, which is but for a moment, is working for us a far more exceeding and eternal weight of glory'

(2 Cor. 4:17).

John Bunyan contrasts our present circumstances with the glories we shall one day experience in that 'better country'.

***Then** shall we have perfect and everlasting visions of God, and that blessed One, his Son, Jesus Christ, a good thought of whom sometimes so fills us while in this world that it causes 'joy unspeakable and full of glory.' **Then** shall our will and affections be ever in a burning flame of love to God and his Son Jesus Christ; our love here has ups and downs, but there it shall be always perfect with that perfection which is not possible in this world to be enjoyed. **Then** will our conscience have that peace and joy that neither tongue, nor pen or men or angels can express. **Then** will our memory be so enlarged to retain all things that happened to us in this world, so that with unspeakable aptness we shall call to mind all God's providences, all Satan's malice, all our own weaknesses, all the rage of men, and how God made all work together for his glory and our good, to the everlasting ravishing of our hearts.*

Saved by Grace, ed. Geoge Offor
Banner of Truth Trust, vol.1, pp. 341-2

'*Now* we see through a glass, darkly; but then face to face: *now*
I know in part; but *then* shall I know even as also I am known'
(1 Cor. 13:12, KJV).

*N*ow an unknown pilgrim pathway,
each tomorrow marred by fears;
then the storm will all be over;
farewell sinning! farewell tears!

Now a moment's light affliction,
now a cross, a life laid down,
then eternal consolation,
robes of splendour and a crown.
Now the op'ning buds of promise,
shyly hid from careless eyes,
then the full-flung flowers of glory,
matchless blooms of Paradise.

Now the ecstasy of longing,
now the life of heaven begun,
then the fulness, *then* the rapture,
then the heart of Jesus won.

Now the discipline of sorrow,
then the gladness and reward;
Now the toil, the guilt, the dying,
then a paradise restored.
Now the vain regrets and turmoil,
then a heart at perfect rest,
now the thirsting, *now* the longing,
then unsullied righteousness.

Now the hope of resurrection,
then a shout of liberty,
death has lost its sting for ever,
swallowed up in victory.

I dare not be so impatient as to beg thee to cut off my time, and snatch me hence unready, because I know my everlasting state so much depends on my improvement in this life. Nor would I stay when my work is done and stay here sinning while my brethren are triumphing ... Lord, I am content to stay thy time and go thy way ... in the meantime, I may desire, but I am not to repine; I may believe and wish though I may not make sinful haste. I am willing to wait for thee, but not to lose thee.

Richard Baxter, *The Saints' Everlasting Rest*

Counting all things loss

'God forbid that I should glory except in the cross of our Lord Jesus Christ, by whom the world has been crucified to me, and I to the world'

(Gal. 6:14).

Behind my back here would I fling
each idol-joy, each subtle chain
that seeks to bind my heaven-born soul
to earth again.

Each dear legitimate desire
I too would render at the cross,
and weeping beg the grace to count
my best as loss.

Life's laughing days, its noblest bliss,
my yearning heart cannot suffice.
But joys undimmed, unmarred I find
only in Christ.

My happiness, my single bliss,
now let me seek in One alone:
the Man of Calvary, my boast —
his cross my throne.

I take you, Jesus

This day I give myself up to thee, a living sacrifice ... in thy service I desire and purpose to spend all my time, desiring thee to teach me to spend every moment of it to thy glory... In that course would I, O Lord, steadfastly persevere to my last breath.

From William Grimshaw of Haworth's
Covenant with God, 4 December 1752,
citing Philip Doddridge's model covenant in his classic
The Rise and Progress of Religion in the Soul

I take you, Jesus:
You only as my soul's delight!
Possess my all, it is your right.
To be the heart of all my bliss,
my hope of fairer worlds than this,
I take you, Jesus.

I take you, Jesus:
Too long have earthly loves held sway,
too long I've feared your better way:
your lonely cross, your thorn-clad brow;
your path of suffering, but now
I take you, Jesus.

I take you, Jesus:
kind Prophet of my wayward soul,
my King to conquer and control,
the Lamb who bears away my stain,
my Priest who cannot plead in vain.
I take you, Jesus.

I take you, Jesus:
my morning ray, my noonday bright,
my star amid the dark'ning night;
as my beloved and my friend
till life's uncertain day shall end,
I take you, JESUS.

If there were ten thousand, thousand millions of worlds, and as many heavens full of men and angels, Christ would not be pinched to supply all our wants and fill us all. Christ is a well of life, but who knows how deep it is to the bottom?

Letters of Samuel Rutherford
Letter 226, Banner of Truth Trust, p. 446

Roses have thorns

Margaret Charlton, a young woman recently converted under Puritan Richard Baxter's preaching in Kidderminster, England, was alarmed to discover a growing love for her pastor, Baxter, a love beyond that due to him as her spiritual guide. But it seemed a forlorn affection, for Baxter was a confirmed bachelor of fifty-eight and Margaret was only twenty-six. More than this, she feared that this heart-attraction was becoming too strong, and that it was taking the place of her newly-found love for God. As she struggled to suppress her feelings, she wrote the following words:

Why should my heart be fixed where my home is not? Heaven is my home; God in Christ is all my happiness. Come, my heart, mount heavenward ... Has not experience taught you that creature-comforts, though they may be roses, have their thorns? O my heart, retire to God, the only satisfying object. There you may love without all danger of excess. Let your love to God be fixed and transcendent.

Margaret's subsequent nineteen-year marriage to Baxter before her death at the age of fifty-five is one of the most beautiful love stories of Puritan times.

*A*nd has this world its magic glades,
its gardens, passing fair,
enchanting bowers that beckon me
to linger here?
Yet veiled beneath the loveliest rose
there lies a hidden thorn,
and hands that grasp the tempting blooms
are quickly torn.

Why should my wayward heart be fixed
on pleasures that must die,
on time's short happiness that fails
to satisfy?
Come then, my soul, and heav'nward mount,
Let earth no more enthrall;
aspire to God, in him to find
your home, your all.

A time will come when Christ will call
his scattered family in;
then farewell sorrow! farewell tears!
and farewell sin!
Then friends shall meet to part no more,
from love's excess set free;
with love transcendent fixed on God,
eternally.

Hope
in days
of darkness

Tested by fire

'He knows the way that I take; when he has tested me, I shall come forth as gold'

(Job 23:10).

Conceived within God's secret thought,
My way was known and planned of old
that in affliction's crucible
he should refine my heart as gold.

His searching flame would now destroy
all taint of base ignoble dross
to fashion for himself at length
a vessel purified by loss.

Yet this I know: though fierce the blaze
(for marred my gold by sin's alloy);
my God has something still in me
no fiery trial can destroy.

O what I owe to the file, to the hammer, to the furnace of my Lord Jesus! who has now let me see how good the wheat of Christ is that goes through his mill and his oven to be made bread for his own table. Grace tried is better than grace, and it is more than grace, it is glory in its infancy ... When Christ blesses his own crosses with a tongue they breathe out Christ's love, wisdom, kindness, and care of us. Why should I start at the plough of my Lord that makes deep furrows on my soul? I know that he is no idle husbandman; he purposes a crop.

Letters of Samuel Rutherford
Banner of Truth Trust, 1984, Letter 76

Horatius Bonar, who lost five of his children in infancy or childhood, described the sufferings of the children of God as the 'family badge'. He could write:

It is good to be afflicted. Our days of suffering here we call days of darkness; hereafter they will seem our brightest and fairest. In eternity we shall praise Jehovah most of all for our sorrows and tears. So blessed shall they then seem to us that we shall wonder how we could ever weep and sigh. We shall then know how utterly unworthy we were of all this grace. We did not deserve anything, but least of all to be afflicted. Our joys were all grace — pure grace — much more our sorrows. It is of the exceeding riches of God's grace that trial comes.

Horatius Bonar, *When God's children suffer*, Kregel, p. 128

The song of the oak

Susanna Spurgeon, wife of C. H. Spurgeon, tells of a dark November night when she was alone in her room. She suddenly thought she could hear a bird singing sweetly somewhere out in the night. But the 'music' was actually coming from an oak log burning in the grate as trapped gases, released by the flames, were escaping.

When the fire of affliction draws songs of praise from us, then indeed we are purified and our God is glorified.

Susannah Spurgeon

A sturdy oak majestic stood
amid the green and changeful wood
and garnered to its oaken heart
a song of summer days:
until grown gnarled and old at last,
that mighty oak was felled and cast
into the fiery blaze
where vehement tongues of flame set free
its long imprisoned melody,
its captured song of praise.

So I, once blessed by favoured years,
now tread a path of pain and tears:
yet with reluctant, stubborn heart
complained against God's ways
until the fires of suffering drew
a hymn of faith, surprising, new,
from trial's scorching blaze.
Then may my God be glorified,
my sinning soul be purified,
by glad submissive praise.

A Christian life is not one constant course but has various changes in it: living and dying, rejoicing and sorrowing, growing and decaying. This is that the manifold wisdom of God and the various graces of his people might appear to keep them unsettled here that they might be in a constant watch ... God is never kinder than when I am under great loads. This is the great advantage of an afflicted state that the Lord pities most and shows most kindness then.

James Fraser of Brea

My God is good

When the Covenanter, Richard Cameron's old father, Allan Cameron, then a prisoner in The Tollbooth, Edinburgh, was shown his son's hands, cruelly severed after his death by one of the King's dragoons after the Battle of Ayrsmoss in 1680, he reacted with words of memorable and courageous faith:

It is the Lord: good is the will of the Lord, who can never wrong me or mine, but has made goodness and mercy to follow us all our days.

Allan Cameron

'Whose hands are these, old man, whose hands?'
with mocking jest, the soldier cried.
The aged prisoner gazed and wept;
'I know them,' he at length replied,
'They are my son's.'

'It is the Lord, the righteous Lord,
who never yet wronged me or mine.
Before his will I meekly bow,
my best, my all, to him resign.
It is the Lord.'

'Good is the Lord and good his will
whose mercies crown my earthly days.
Beyond the pain, eternal joy,
beyond the tears, unceasing praise.
My Lord is good.'

Lord, I accept

'Then Jacob was left alone; and a man wrestled with him until the breaking of day. Now when he saw that he did not prevail against him, he touched … the socket of Jacob's hip … Then Jacob asked, saying, "Tell me your name, I pray." And he said, "Why is it that you ask about my name?" And he blessed him there'

(Genesis 32:24-25a, 29).

*L*ord, I accept:
the numbing pain, the rending grief,
the drooping bud and withered leaf
of time's fair joys; the path of loss,
the way of sorrow and the cross,
these I accept.

Lord, I accept:
but not without a weary fight
as Jacob through the bitter night
strove with his God, until at length
the God of mercy broke his strength
and mastered him.

Lord, I accept:
but torn with grief my untamed will
dared not obey or yield until
with anguish that no tongue can tell
he slew the joys I loved so well
and conquered me.

Now I accept.
Though vanquished I may triumphs gain,
new hopes distil from loss and pain;
like Jacob, let me hence prevail
and drink of joys that cannot fail
or ever die.

I was made to see that if ever I would suffer rightly I must first pass a sentence of death upon everything that can properly be called a thing of this life — even to reckon myself, my wife, my children, my health, my enjoyments and all as dead to me and myself as dead to them. The second was to live upon God who is invisible.

John Bunyan, *Grace Abounding to the Chief of Sinners,* paras. 324-5

Troubles will be no troubles, distresses will be no distresses if you can but secure the presence of God with you. God's signal presence will turn storms into calm, winter nights into summer days, prisons into palaces. No afflictions, no trials can make it night with the Christian so long as he enjoys the presence of God with his spirit. God's gracious presence makes every condition to be a little heaven to the believing soul.

Thomas Brooks
The Signal Presence of God with his People in their Greatest Troubles
vol. 5, p. 568

The power
of prayer

In prayer we may plead the sorrows of God's people — Jeremiah is the great master of this art. He talks of all their griefs and calls upon the Lord to look upon his suffering Zion, and ere long his plaintive cries are heard. Nothing so eloquent with the father as his child's cry ... Ah! When God's Israel shall be brought very low so that they can scarcely cry, then comes the Lord's time of deliverance, and he is sure to show that he loves his people. Whenever you see a church brought very low you may use her griefs as an argument why God should return and save the remnant of his people.

C. H. Spurgeon
Order and argument in Prayer
New Park Street Pulpit, vol. 12

How long, O, Lord?

'How long, O LORD? Will you forget me for ever? How long will you hide your face from me? How long shall I take counsel in my soul, having sorrow in my heart daily?'

(Psalm 13:1).

'How long, O Lord, how long?'
the ceaseless cry
of suffering saints who plead and wait
with tireless faith at heaven's gate,
nor dare depart till heard on high;
'O Lord, how long?'

'How long, O Lord, how long?'
the humble cry
of those who wrestle to believe
although no answer they receive,
nor kindly smile, they know not why:
'O Lord, how long?'

'How long, O Lord, how long?'
the broken cry
of hearts long torn by baffling pain,
that find all earthly comfort vain,
and heav'nward turn with troubled sigh:
'O Lord, how long?'

'Not long, my child, not long,'
comes heaven's reply
to those who will not be denied,
to those who have no hope beside;
'I shake the earth, I rend the sky,
I come ere long.'

In *The Privy Key of Heaven* Thomas Brooks gives words of consolation especially to those who fear that God's delay in answering prayer means that their requests are unheard.

Though God delays, yet he does not forget you. He remembers you still; you are still in his eye and always upon his heart ... God's time is always the best time ... to set God his time is to limit him, it is to exalt ourselves above him as if we were wiser than God ... He delayed Joseph long but at length he changed his iron fetters into chains of gold, his rags into royal robes, his prison into a palace, his reproach into honour and his thirty years of suffering into eighty years reigning in much grandeur and splendour.

God delays that his people may set upon him with greater strength and importunity; he puts them off that they may put [him] on with greater life and vigour. God seems cold that he may make us more hot. He seems slack that he may make us more earnest. He seems backward that he may make us more pressing in our demands upon him. God aims by all his 'put-offs' that his children may send up more honourable prayers after him; that they may cry the more earnestly, strive more mightily, and wrestle more importunately with God and that they may take heaven with a more sacred violence. So when a Christian prays and prays and yet God seems silent and heaven seems shut against him, yet let him not cast off prayer, but mend his prayer. Let him pray more believingly, more affectionately and pray more fervently and then mercy will come and comfort will come and deliverance will come.

Watchmen on the walls

'I have set watchmen on your walls, O Jerusalem; they shall never hold their peace day or night. You who make mention of the LORD, do not keep silent, and give him no rest till he establishes and till he makes Jerusalem a praise in the earth'

(Isaiah 62:6-7).

On Zion's broken battlements
her watchmen stand;
See how they gaze with grieving eyes
upon the land.
For Zion, once so fair, so strong
a ruin lies;
her enemies with mocking scorn
her God despise.

And can her watchmen silent stand
before the sight?
Ah no, with burdened hearts they cry
both day and night.
With upraised arms and wakeful eyes
in deep distress
to heaven their ceaseless prayers ascend,
nor can they rest.

How long must Zion wasted lie,
her glory dead?
How long in desolation sunk,
her comforts fled?
O Lord our God, return again!
Behold our need;
make your afflicted people glad
the watchmen plead.

O Zion, grieving and forlorn,
I shall arise,
My changeless promise to fulfil
before your eyes.
No more will I forsake your land,
nor will I rest
until your beauty and my grace
stand manifest.

A crown of glory you shall be
in my own hand.
Salvation like a blazing torch
shall light your land.
To you shall every nation flow
your God to praise,
you shall be called 'the Lord's delight'
through endless days.

Have we got a vision of what the church is meant to be? Do we see the contrast between our present state and what she can and will be? If we have, let us set watchmen on the walls. Let us become the Lord's remembrancers in every sense of the term. And let us take no rest and let us give him no rest until Jerusalem shall again become a praise and a glory, and her brightness and her righteousness shall shine.

D. M. Lloyd-Jones
Revival — Can we make it happen?
Marshall Pickering, p. 262

'Ask, and it will be given to you; seek, and you will find; knock, and it will be opened to you. For everyone who asks receives, and he who seeks finds, and to him who knocks it will be opened'
(Matthew 7:7-8).

Wordless prayer

'Lord, all my desire is before you, and my sighing is not hidden from you'

(Psalm 38:9).

With strong desires would I draw near,
before your throne bowed low.
O turn to me your listening ear;
to whom else may I go?

Yet language with its utmost art
but poorly can express
the longings of a burdened heart,
its tale of bitterness.

A stumbling prayer, a tear, a groan,
O Christ, is all I bring;
Searcher of souls, do not disdain
this broken offering.

My guilt, my sins, my desperate need
call out with silent tongue;
O turn me not away I plead,
but let a sinner come.

Dumbly I wait with aching heart,
dumbly for you I cry,
nor will I from your throne depart
till I am heard on high.

Then for the sake of One who prayed
with tears and crying strong,
kind God arise, send down your aid
and turn my grief to song.

God's dearest children may sometimes be so shut up that they have been able to say nothing, nor to do anything but groan. A child of God may sometimes meet with such a blow from God, from conscience, from Scripture, from Satan, from the world that may for a time so astonish him that he may not be able to speak to God, nor speak to others, nor speak to his own heart... The force, the virtue, the efficacy, the excellency of prayer does not consist in the number and flourish of words, but in the supernatural motions of the Spirit, in sighs and groans and pangs and strong affections of the heart that are unspeakable and unutterable. Certainly, the very soul of prayer lies in the pouring out of a man's soul before the Lord, though it be but in sighs, groans and tears.

Thomas Brooks
Works, *The Privy Key of Heaven*, vol.2, pp. 221-2

John Bunyan also gives valuable help for believers when prayer seems hard:

The best prayers have often more groans than words, and those words that it has are but lean and shallow representations of the heart, life and spirit of that prayer ... God is the God of spirits and his eyes look further than at the outside of any duty whatsoever ... The nearer a man comes in any work that God commands him to do, according to his will, so much the more hard and difficult it is.

Prayer
Banner of Truth Trust, 1965, pp. 32-3

The intercessors

'I sought for a man among them who would … stand in the gap
before me on behalf of the land, that I should not destroy it; but
I found no one'

(Ezekiel 22:30).

'He saw that there was no man, and wondered that there was no
intercessor'

(Isaiah 59:16).

I looked for one to stand within the gap,
to seek my mercy in an evil day;
to plead that I might sheathe my outstretched sword,
and turn my wrath away.

I searched for such a one, but all in vain;
for none would bear the intercessor's part —
too busy far to understand or share
the burden of my heart.

Then must I pour upon a godless land
those vials of chastisement so long delayed,
or bring at last that judgment still restrained
because no one has prayed?

Wait Lord! Hold back that wrath so well deserved,
a little longer spare a sinning land;
for here is one, though faltering, who dares
within the gap to stand.

Just one? Ah no, another, and yet more!
We hear the cry and now rise up at last
to plead for pardon, ere it is too late,
or mercy's day is past.

By strong beseeching in the silent night,
in stolen moments through the active day,
with weeping hearts we call upon our God
to turn his wrath away.

In an astonishing passage on the nature and power of true prayer, C. H. Spurgeon says:

Prayer is the grandest power in the entire universe; it has a more omnipotent force than electricity, attraction, gravitation or any other of those secret forces which men have called by names, but which they do not understand. Prayer has as palpable, as true, as sure, as invariable an influence over the entire universe as any of the laws of nature. When a man really prays it is not a question whether God will hear him or not, he must hear him; not because there is any compulsion in the prayer, but there is a sweet and blessed compulsion in the promise. God has promised to hear prayer and he will perform his promise. As he is the most high and true God, he cannot deny himself. Oh! To think of this; that you, a puny creature, may stand here and speak to God, and through God may move all the worlds. Yet when your prayer is heard, creation will not be disturbed though the grandest ends be answered, providence will not be disarranged for a single moment. No leaf will fall earlier from the tree, not a star will stay in its course, nor one drop of water trickle more slowly from its fount; all will go on the same, yet your prayer will have affected everything. It will speak to the decrees and purposes of God as they are being daily fulfilled ... Our prayers are God's decrees in another shape; the prayers of God's people are but God's promises breathed out of living hearts, and those promises are the decrees, only put into another form and fashion.

You have power in prayer and you stand today among the most potent ministers in the universe God has made ... The ear of God himself will listen and the hand of God himself will yield to your will. There is nothing, I repeat, there is no force so tremendous, no energy so marvellous, as the energy with which God has endowed every man, who like Jacob can wrestle, like Israel can prevail with him in prayer. Unless the Eternal will swerve from his word, unless the oath which he has given shall be revoked, and he himself shall cease to be what he is, 'We know we have the petitions that we desired of him.'

True Prayer ... True Power
New Park Street Pulpit, vol. 6

The God of promise

Stir up your strength

'Give ear, O Shepherd of Israel ... stir up your strength, and come and save us! ... How long will you be angry against the prayer of your people? ... Restore us, O God of hosts; cause your face to shine, and we shall be saved!'

(Psalm 80).

Shepherd of Israel, omnipotent Saviour,
stir up your strength and arise to our need:
stand not afar from your people's oppression,
look down from heaven and save us we plead.

Is this the vineyard your right hand has planted,
prospered and blessed by the strength of your might?
See her forsaken, uprooted and plundered,
mocked and despised in her pitiful plight.

Kind God of glory, return in your mercy,
favour us now with the smiles of your face.
Shine from above till our hearts meek and chastened
cling to our God through the help of your grace.

Shepherd of Israel, omnipotent Saviour,
stir up your strength and revive us once more!
Then shall we call on that name all-majestic,
nor turn again from the God we adore.

A day shall dawn

'There shall be a day when the watchmen will cry on Mount Ephraim, "Arise, and let us go up to Zion, to the Lord our God." For thus says the Lord: "... Behold, I will bring them from the north country, and gather them from the ends of the earth... Therefore they shall come and sing in the height of Zion ... the young men and the old, together ... and my people shall be satisfied with my goodness"'

(Jeremiah 31:6-14).

A day shall dawn: like music on our hearing,
the promise sounds across the restless years —
a day of days; a day of God's appearing,
when songs and laughter shall supplant our tears.

That day draws near! Tell out the news with gladness,
O watchmen on the lonely mountain bare:
whose eyes have searched the barren wastes with sadness,
whose arms reached up in interceding prayer.

God's day draws near! Rejoice in hope, O mourners:
the missing ones shall be brought in ere long!
A mighty host from earth's remotest corners
in Zion's height shall join in endless song:

From north and south with mirth surpassing telling,
both young and old in dancing shall rejoice;
content at last — their utmost praises swelling,
proclaim God's goodness with untiring voice!

John Knox's dying prayer:

I have been in meditation these last two nights upon the troubled kirk of God, despised of the world but precious in his sight and have called to God for it, and commended it to Christ her head. I have been fighting against Satan who is ever ready to assault. I have fought against spiritual wickedness and have prevailed.

He died the following day, 23 November 1572.

The hope of Israel

'O Hope of Israel, his Saviour in time of trouble, why should you be like a stranger in the land, and like a traveller who turns aside to tarry for a night? ... We are called by your name; do not leave us! ... Do not disgrace the throne of your glory!'

(Jeremiah 14:8, 9, 21).

O God, the Hope of Israel,
our only friend,
kind Saviour in a troubled hour,
to us attend;
for we are called by your great name;
do not disgrace
your throne of glory in our midst,
or hide your face.

The burden of our guilt and sin
declares our need;
no worthiness have we to boast
or righteous deed.
Backsliding hearts and faltering love
we sadly own,
yet rest our earnest heav'nward plea
on grace alone.

Why should our God seem far removed
beyond our prayer?
Why like a stranger in the land
must he appear;
or like a traveller who stays
just for a night,
to journey on his pilgrim way
at morning light?

O may the Hope of Israel
our prayers receive,
nor like the hasty sojourner
his people leave.
Then for his glory and our peace
we now implore
our God to tarry long with us,
at home once more.

A foretaste

*O*nce I felt God's day arising —
felt him drawing near:
glory trembling on the threshold,
singing in the air.

Yes, I sipped the wine of heaven —
I can taste it yet!
Sweet intoxicating gladness —
how can I forget?

Must these lips that tasted glory
thirsting still remain?
Can the heart that sensed his dawning
rest content again?

No, my soul, arise pursue him:
never let him go.
Pour your heart's complaint before him,
emptiness and woe.

Show the need, the thirst, the longing,
grief too deep for tears;
plead his people's desolation,
plead the barren years.

Rise then, O my God in glory;
rend the heavens apart;
demonstrate your might and mercy
to the yearning heart.

Let the God of power accomplish
love's fair work begun;
bring your day-spring's glad fulfilment —
let your kingdom come!

Compare the joy which you shall have in heaven with what the saints have found in the way to it, and in the foretastes of it. Has not God sometimes revealed himself extraordinarily to your soul and let a drop of glory fall upon it? Have you not been ready to say, 'O that it might be thus with my soul continually?' ... What [then] will my joys be when my soul shall be so capable of seeing and enjoying God, that though the light be a thousand times greater than the sun, yet my eyes shall be able for ever to behold it.

Richard Baxter, *The Saints' Everlasting Rest*

The God of promise

*S*trong God of promise, I will trust
your word that timeless shall endure
till mountains crumble into dust
and are no more.

This word of promise came to me,
a promise from the heart of God,
engraved from all eternity
in wounds and blood.

'My church I build, so fair, so great,
no force against her shall prevail.
Before her even hell's foul gate
must bow and fail.'

Here let me stand: this I believe,
though all may scorn, though Satan mock:
to this sure promise I will cleave,
a changeless rock.

Yet lest I doubt, the God of might
has drawn his pledge across the sky,
to preach in rainbow colours bright,
'I cannot lie.'

THE GOD OF PROMISE

His faithful word spans earth and skies,
vast as the rainbow's wide embrace,
declares before my longing eyes
the power of grace.

The hope
of glory

The Lily of the Valleys

'I am ... the lily of the valleys'

(Song of Solomon 2:1).

The following words were written for my father, Stanley Rowe, who experienced a long and grievous journey through 'the valley of the shadow of death'. The enemy of souls assaulted him fiercely, pointing to his sins and robbing him of assurance of forgiveness. Heaven seemed a frightening and forbidding concept even to one who had spent his entire life in missionary service, pointing others heavenward. These lines were written in an attempt to console him and lift his spirits, though he was probably too ill to grasp their meaning. However, the Saviour himself comforted him shortly before the end, assuring him that he was 'able to keep him from falling' and would 'present him faultless before the presence of his glory with exceeding joy'.

'Yea, though I walk through the valley of the shadow of death, I will fear no evil: for thou art with me...'

(Psalm 23:4, KJV).

*C*hrist, the Lily of the Valleys,
Son of God in meekness clad,
flowering in the soil of sorrows,
consolation of the sad;
shyly hidden by the wayside,
veiled from unbelieving eyes,
springs in unassuming beauty,
Christ, the Flower of Paradise.

Dark this valley of my weeping
stretched along my pilgrim way;
broken hopes and wistful longings;
tears by night and fears by day.
Can the lily of the valleys
flourish in such hostile ground?
Faith can see with eyes of wonder
lilies everywhere around!

Under thorn and threat'ning bramble,
near each boulder of despair,
see, the lily of the valleys
bows in lowly fragrance there.
Bright amid the stony wasteland,
clothed in radiance, pure and white;
So may Christ, in radiant beauty,
shine into my gath'ring night.

When I tread that last dark valley
through the shades of fearsome death,
wage that final, bitter warfare
ere I yield my falt'ring breath
I shall find the Christ of glory
ever to my heart more dear,
find the Lily of the Valleys
hid in many a crevice there.

Charles Spurgeon wrote words of consolation for those walking through the valley of the shadow of death:

> *Observe that it is not walking in the valley but through the valley. We go through the dark tunnel of death and emerge into the light of immortality. We do not die, we do but sleep to wake in glory. Death is not the house but the porch, not the goal but the passage to it. Dying is called a 'valley'. The storm breaks on the mountain but the valley is a place of quietude … the mountain is bleak and bare, but the valley is rich with golden sheaves, and many a saint has reaped more knowledge when he came to die than he ever knew when he lived. Death stands by the side of the highway, and the light of heaven shining upon him throws a light across our path; let us then rejoice that there is a light beyond. The shadow of a dog cannot bite; the shadow of a sword cannot kill; the shadow of death cannot destroy us.*
>
> *The Treasury of David*
> vol. 1, p. 401

Heaven is a place where all joy is enjoyed: mirth without sadness, light without darkness, sweetness without bitterness, rest without labour, plenty without poverty, life without death. O what joy enters into a believer when he enters into the joy of his Saviour! Who would not work for glory with the greatest diligence and wait for glory with the greatest patience? O what glories there are in glory — to be in Christ is heaven below, to be with Christ is heaven above.

William Grimshaw of Haworth

My Father's house

These lines were written at the death of a dear friend who left a note saying, 'Do not grieve for me for I am still in my Father's house.'

Grieve not for me when I shall mount
nearer to him whose face I love;
grieve not for me, for I but change
this room below for one above,
still in my Father's house.

There will my changeful spirit rest,
there will I find a settled home;
weary of straying out and in,
my wayward feet no more will roam
far from my Father's house.

So do not grieve — yet if you weep
let joy and longing blend your tears,
till you shall rise to join with me
beyond the land of grief and cares —
safe in our Father's house.

He has fought a good fight, he has finished the course, he has kept the faith ... His battle is over, and then for him there is rest and home. Home! Yes, home. A home prepared from the foundation of the world, a home in the many mansions, a home in the innermost circle of creation, nearest the throne and heart of God, a home whose peace shall never be broken by the sound of war or tempest, whose brightness shall never be overcast by the remotest shadow of a cloud. How solacing ... to think of a resting place so near, and that resting place our Father's house.

When God's children suffer
Horatius Bonar, Kregel Publications, p. 131

The conqueror of death

'O death, where is your sting? O Hades, where is your victory? The sting of death is sin, and the strength of sin is the law. But thanks be to God who gives us the victory through our Lord Jesus Christ'

(1 Cor. 15:55-7).

Phillip Saphir, older brother of Adolph Saphir, was one of the five children of an orthodox and highly respected Jewish family converted to Christ as their true Messiah in a unusual work of God in Budapest (then known as Pesth) during the early 1840s. At the age of twenty-three Phillip was taken terminally ill with cancer, dying five years later in 1849. He suffered greatly but out of the fire of affliction was able to write:

My whole body is ruined. In heaven there will be no pain. I praise the Lamb slain for us... God has done great things for me. I am happy; my body is decaying... but within I am strong in God and rich in him who became poor for me. Heat takes away the dross and prepares a transcendent joy. I do not dread to die; the Conqueror of death has taken away its sting.

O Conqueror of death and hell,
O Lamb for sinners slain,
Come, set my life above the reach
and tyranny of pain.
For ruined stands this earthly house,
my tenement of clay,
as I await my house from heaven —
beyond decay.

Strong in my God and rich in him
no more I dread to die,
for pain is but the instrument
to sift and purify.
Then let affliction's scorching heat
all taint of dross destroy;
prepare my soul to comprehend
transcendent joy.

The land of my desires

'Now they desire a better, that is, a heavenly country'
(Hebrews 11:16).

The Christian is never wholly separated from the land of promise. His tents are pitched in close view of the city of God. Heaven is present to the believer's experience in no less real a sense than Canaan with its fair hills and valleys lay close to the vision of Abraham. As Abraham breathed the air of Canaan, he was given to taste the powers of the world to come and was refreshed. The roots of the Christian's life are fed from those rich perennial springs that lie deep in the recesses of converse with God, where prayers ascend and divine graces descend, so that after each season of tryst he issues, a new man, from the secrecy of his tent.

Geerhardus Vos
Grace and Glory
Banner of Truth Trust, 1994
pp. 111-2, 115

*A*s flowers turning seek the light,
as rivers hasten to the sea,
so deep within believing hearts
earth cries aloud for heaven,
and time pleads for eternity.

A pilgrim and a sojourner,
a stranger in this place of tears,
my eyes have glimpsed, though from afar,
a better country and a fairer home
beyond these fleeting years.

True homeland of the heav'n-born soul —
destined for immortality —
its crystal streams, its verdant fields,
unmarred and undefiled by sin,
forever beckon me.

Toward the land of my desires,
then let me pitch my pilgrim tent,
deaf to the clamouring charms of earth;
to wait in hope that better dawn
with cheerful discontent.

Yet now and then with eagle flight
my faith would upward soar to bring,
fresh from that bright utopia
some balm to soothe the homesick heart
on its returning wing!

Samuel Rutherford, the Scottish Covenanter, taken from his home and church in Anwoth, Galloway, was put under house-arrest in Aberdeen in 1636. To him the longing for that 'better country' was often intense and one that he frequently expressed in his letters from exile.

The sum of glory will take you and all the angels telling [to unfold]. We but dwell here because we can do no better. It is need, not virtue, to be sojourners in a prison; to weep, and sigh and, alas! to sin sixty or seventy years in a land of tears. The fruits that grow here are all seasoned and salted with sin... It were a well-spent journey to creep hands and feet through seven deaths and seven hells, to enjoy him [Christ] up at the well-head. Only let us not weary, the miles to that land are fewer and shorter than when we first believed. Strangers are not wise to quarrel with their host, and complain of their lodging. It is a foul way, but a fair home. Oh! that I had such grapes and clusters out of that land as I have sometimes seen and tasted.

Letters of Samuel Rutherford
Banner of Truth Trust, 1984, Letter 318

Look up!

*L*ook up, O suffering child of grace!
How short is sorrow's day!
You soon shall reign
and glory gain
where tears are wiped away.

ℬeulah land

'Your eyes will behold the King in his beauty; they will see a land that stretches afar'

(Isaiah 33:17, ESV).

'Your land [shall be called] Beulah'

(Isaiah 62:4).

Now I saw in my dream that by this time the pilgrims were ... entering the country of Beulah, whose air was very sweet and pleasant... Yea, here they heard continually the singing of birds, and saw every day the flowers appear in the earth... In this country the sun shineth night and day; wherefore this was beyond the valley of the Shadow of death... Here they were within sight of the city they were going to...

The Pilgrim's Progress, Part 2

Were I to adopt the figurative language of Bunyan, I might date this letter, 'From the Land of Beulah' of which I have been for some weeks a happy inhabitant... The celestial city is full in my view. Its glories beam upon me, its breezes fan me, its odours are wafted to me, its sounds strike upon my ears, and its spirit is breathed into my heart. Nothing separates me from it but the river of death, which now appears but an insignificant rill, that may be crossed at a single step whenever God shall give permission.

Edward Payson's last letter to his sister

*F*air Beulah land! Blest land where now I dwell;
one tongue is not enough to tell
its joys sufficiently.
I see the City full in sight,
I bask in beams of glory-light;
the Sun of Righteousness draws near
irradiates my hemisphere
with shining purity.
So close this land to heaven's gate
at times my heart can scarcely wait
till Christ shall beckon me.

Fair Beulah land! Nor could I think before
such hidden wonders lay in store
for Christians when they die.
I breathe its fragrant heavenly air,
celestial music fills my ear,
pervading all my wakeful dreams,
and even death's dark river seems
to lose its dread that I
may cross it at a single pace
to greet my Saviour face to face
beyond the brightening sky.